U.S.A.
Constitution
Activity Book

Tony J. Tallarico

DOVER PUBLICATIONS, INC.
Mineola, New York

Often referred to as the "supreme law of the land," the Constitution of the United States outlines the power of the government, as well as the ways that the government should be limited in order to protect the rights of United States citizens. In this fact-filled activity book, you will learn about both the history and the contents of the United States Constitution, as you meet the challenges of word scrambles, word searches, mazes, codes, find-the-differences, and many other entertaining puzzles. Solutions begin on page 37. After you have completed the activities, you can color in the pages with colored pencils or markers.

Bibliographical Note

U.S.A. Constitution Activity Book is a new work,
first published by Dover Publications, Inc., in 2016.

International Standard Book Number

ISBN-13: 978-0-486-80934-2
ISBN-10: 0-486-80934-X

Manufactured in the United States by LSC Communications
80934X09   2018
www.doverpublications.com

Amendments

In 1791, Congress ratified 10 amendments (or changes) to the Constitution that outlined the basic rights and freedoms of American citizens.
What is the term for these amendments?
Circle all the letters that contain a star ✳. Then list these letters, in the order they appear, in the spaces below to learn the answer.

T	A	H	D	L	E	S	B
M	I	L	N	L	H	U	O
F	T	R	E	I	J	G	K
C	H	O	S	T	E	R	S

___ ___ ___

___ ___ ___ ___ ___ ___ ___

___ ___ ___ ___ ___ ___

Articles

The Constitution is divided into seven articles, or sections, each addressing a different topic.
Find and circle the listed words having to do with these articles in the puzzle below.
(The words can appear horizontally, vertically, diagonally, and backwards.)

BILLS
BRANCH
COMMERCE
CONGRESS
EXECUTIVE
FEDERAL
GUIDELINES
HOUSE
JUDICIAL
LEGISLATIVE
OATH
POWER
PRESIDENT
PROTECT
SENATE
STATES
SUPPORT
SUPREME COURT
VOTE

```
E  V  I  T  A  L  S  I  G  E  L
V  S  T  I  V  B  C  D  U  C  A
S  R  E  W  O  P  O  W  I  R  I
U  S  A  S  T  E  D  I  D  E  C
P  L  A  R  E  D  E  F  E  M  I
R  A  L  D  R  T  S  S  L  M  D
E  O  T  H  A  N  L  O  I  O  U
M  E  X  N  N  L  L  J  N  C  J
E  X  E  C  U  T  I  V  E  O  V
C  S  I  T  U  C  B  N  S  N  R
O  R  U  L  E  G  I  C  S  G  B
U  P  R  O  T  E  C  T  T  R  A
R  U  O  C  H  S  U  E  A  E  J
T  R  O  P  P  U  S  N  T  S  B
S  L  I  B  P  S  C  F  E  S  R
H  C  O  A  T  H  E  V  S  U  G
T  N  E  D  I  S  E  R  P  R  T
```

Before the Constitution

In 1776, the 13 colonies declared themselves free from Great Britain and became the United States of America. The young country initially developed a document that served as its first constitution. What was it called? Unscramble a synonym for each of these words. (Synonyms are words that mean nearly the same thing, like JOYOUS and MERRY.) Once you have unscrambled them, write the numbered letters in their correct order below to complete the answer.

HALT ☞ T O S P

—— — —— —
11 1 25

SHOW ☞ L I S D P Y A

—— — — — — —— —
19 7   9 22

QUIET ☞ L E E P A C U F

— —— — —— —— —— — —
  20 4 14 3 13

BENT ☞ O R K E D C O

— —— —— —— — —— —
8 21 12 15   10

CORRECT ☞ I G T R H

— —— — —— ——
5 24   2 6

HUMOROUS ☞ Y F N U N

—— — —— —— —
17   26 16

TINY ☞ E T T I L L

— — —— — — ——
    23   18

—— —— ——   —— —— —— —— —— —— ——   —— ——
1 2 3   4 5 6 7 8 9 10 11   12 13

—— —— —— —— —— —— —— —— —— —— —— —— ——
14 15 16 17 18 19 20 21 22 23 24 25 26

3

Constitution Day

Constitution Day is normally celebrated on September 17. When it falls on a weekend or on a holiday, schools and other institutions observe the holiday on an adjacent weekday.

Although first recognized in 1911, what year was Constitution Day established by law?

Using a pencil, darken in the areas that contain a dot ● to reveal the answer.

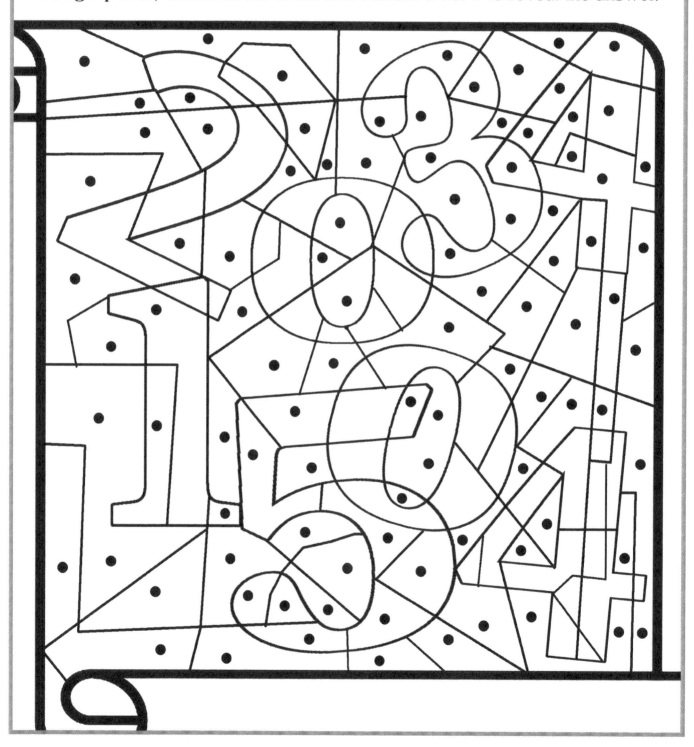

FAMOUS SIGNERS

Signers of the Constitution included some of the greatest names in early American history.
Correctly travel through this maze to reach the person who did NOT sign.

BENJAMIN FRANKLIN

GEORGE WASHINGTON

THOMAS JEFFERSON

JAMES MADISON

Federalist Papers

James Madison and Alexander Hamilton wrote a series of essays to persuade people to approve the Constitution. The 85 essays, published in newspapers across the states in 1787, were known as the "Federalist Papers." Which statesman and patriot from New York City helped Madison and Hamilton write these articles?

To learn his name, cross out each letter that appears THREE times in this puzzle grid. List the remaining letters, in the order they appear, in the blank spaces below.

	S	E	J	I	O	
B	H	T	R	N	S	I
M	E	J	B	V	T	M
T	V	R	S	A	V	B
	I	Y	E	M	R	

_ _ _ _   _ _ _

First American

One of the Founding Fathers of the U.S., Benjamin Franklin was an author, printer, politician, postmaster, inventor, and scientist. He earned the title of "The First American" for his devoted work in uniting the colonies in the years leading up to the Revolutionary War. Franklin is one of the few Fathers who signed both the Declaration of Independence and the Constitution.
Fill in this wall by using only the letters in the top name BEN to complete the 10 words below. Some letters may be used more than once in a word.

First National Thanksgiving

A proclamation by President George Washington and a congressional resolution established the first national Thanksgiving Day on Nov. 26, 1789.
What was the reason for the holiday?
Use the chart below to decode the answer.

It had nothing to do with pumpkin pie!

	a	b	c	d	e	f
1	G	K	O	H	R	B
2	S	A	F	I	W	U
3	E	T	V	N	C	J

__ __   __ __ __ __
3b 1c   1a 2d 3c 3a

__ __ __ __ __ __   __ __ __
3b 1d 2b 3d 1b 2a   2c 1c 1e

__ __ __   __ __ __
3b 1d 3a   3d 3a 2e

__ __ __ __ __ __ __ __ __ __ __ __ .
3e 1c 3d 2a 3b 2d 3b 2f 3b 2d 1c 3d

8

First State

Which was the first state to ratify the Constitution?
Write the names of these U.S. states in their correct spaces. The circled letters,
once listed below in the order they appear, will spell out the answer.

ALASKA
CALIFORNIA
MAINE
MONTANA
NEW HAMPSHIRE
RHODE ISLAND

December 7, 1787

— — — — — — — — — —

Framers

The delegates present at the Constitutional Convention were also referred to as Framers of the Constitution.
Draw a line from each picture on the left to its twin on the right.

Influential Delegate

Representing New York, this writer, lawyer and Revolutionary War soldier was just 30 years old when he signed the Constitution. One of the most influential interpreters and promoters of the document, he later served as the first U.S. Secretary of the Treasury.

To learn his name, first circle these words in the puzzle below. The letters that remain, once listed in the order they appear, will spell out his name.

AMBITIOUS   ASSEMBLYMAN   BRAVE
CAREER   DELEGATE   HUSBAND
LAWYER   LEADER   MILITARY
PATRIOT   POLITICIAN   SMART
SOLDIER   TRUE   WRITER

P	O	L	I	T	I	C	I	A	N
A	D	N	A	B	S	U	H	C	A
T	T	R	U	E	A	L	E	A	M
R	X	M	I	L	I	T	A	R	Y
I	R	L	A	N	D	E	R	E	L
O	E	E	V	A	R	B	H	E	B
T	I	A	W	R	I	T	E	R	M
R	D	D	E	L	E	G	A	T	E
A	L	E	A	M	I	L	T	O	S
M	O	R	E	Y	W	A	L	N	S
S	S	U	O	I	T	I	B	M	A

_ _ _ _ _ _ _ _

_ _ _ _ _ _ _ _ _

In the Beginning

Although Americans celebrate the fourth of July and the signing of the Declaration of Independence as the beginning of our country, the real birth of our nation took place in 1787.

Circle the EVEN numbered letters in this puzzle. Then list these letters, in the order they appear, in the spaces below to complete the sentence.

16	5	4	22	11	6	3	14	20	13	2
D	A	E	L	I	E	B	G	A	S	T
21	8	31	10	24	12	18	1	7	26	9
R	E	Y	S	C	O	U	M	H	N	D
16	8	14	7	6	11	12	4	10	29	2
T	R	Y	F	G	P	A	T	H	W	E
28	1	32	12	5	22	26	3	8	16	30
R	V	E	D	K	C	O	L	N	S	T
2	10	4	7	12	11	6	16	15	8	13
I	T	U	Q	T	A	I	O	E	N	S

O N   S E P T E M B E R   1 7 ,   1 7 8 7

_ _ _ _ _ _ _ _ _   F R O M   A L L

O V E R   T H E   _ _ _ _ _ _ _

_ _ _ _ _ _ _   T O   S I G N

T H E   _ _ _ _ _ _ _ _ _ _ _ _

O F   T H E   U N I T E D   S T A T E S .

Jacob Shallus

The Constitution was "penned" by a Pennsylvania General Assembly clerk
named Jacob Shallus. An engrosser (or penman), Shallus handwrote the
4-page document onto parchment over the course of one weekend.
How much was he paid?
Fill in the areas that contain this symbol ✳ to reveal the answer.

JAMES MADISON

James Madison is often referred to as the "Father of the Constitution" because many of his ideas made their way into the document. A statesman and political theorist, he later served as America's 4th president.
Which two pictures of James Madison are exactly the same?
Find and circle them.

1.

2.

3.

4.

5.

6.

Lawyer and Statesman

A Founding Father of the United States, this representative from Connecticut was the only person to sign all four great state papers of the U.S.: the Continental Association, the Declaration of Independence, the Articles of Confederation, and the Constitution.
To learn his name, write the listed words into the grid in alphabetical order. The third letter from each word will spell out his name.

JUST

EGGS

TINY

PART

CART

HURT

SAME

KOHL

DOOR

SEAL

MEET

FREE

Madison's Plan

While waiting for the Convention to formally begin in Philadelphia, James Madison sketched out his initial draft of the Constitution. What was it called? Travel through this maze to discover the answer.

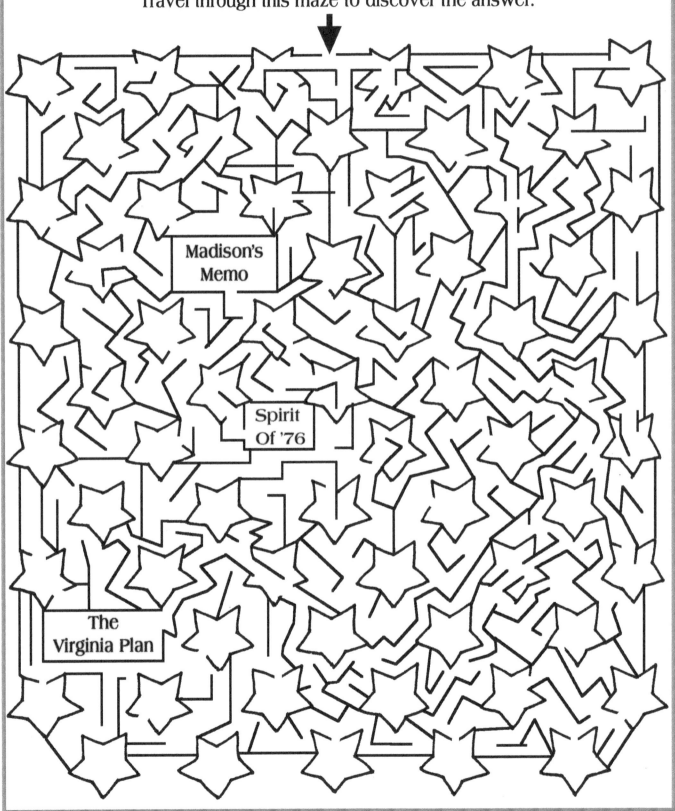

Not Born in the USA

Representing New Jersey, this signer of the U.S. Constitution was born in County Antrim, Ireland. When he was almost 2 years of age, his family emigrated to America.
Correctly travel through this maze to discover his name.

William
Livingston

William
Paterson

William C.
Houston

Official Start

The government under the U.S. Constitution officially began on what date?
Travel through this maze by choosing the path made up of only letters
from the word CONSTITUTION.

On Display

Since 1952, the original Constitution has been kept on display. It is preserved in a case that contains argon gas and is kept at 67 degrees Fahrenheit. To find out where this historical document is located, fill in the blanks with their correct missing vowels, A E I O U.

TH_ N_T__N_L

_RCH_V_S

B__LD_NG

L_C_T_D

N_RTH _F TH_

N_T__N_L M_LL

_N

W_SH_NGT_N, D.C.

Opposed the Constitution

Best known for his speeches about independence, this Founding Father surprisingly did NOT sign the Constitution. He feared it endangered the rights of states as well as the freedoms of individuals. (He did later help gain approval for the Bill of Rights.)

Write the name of each object pictured. One letter from each will spell out his name.

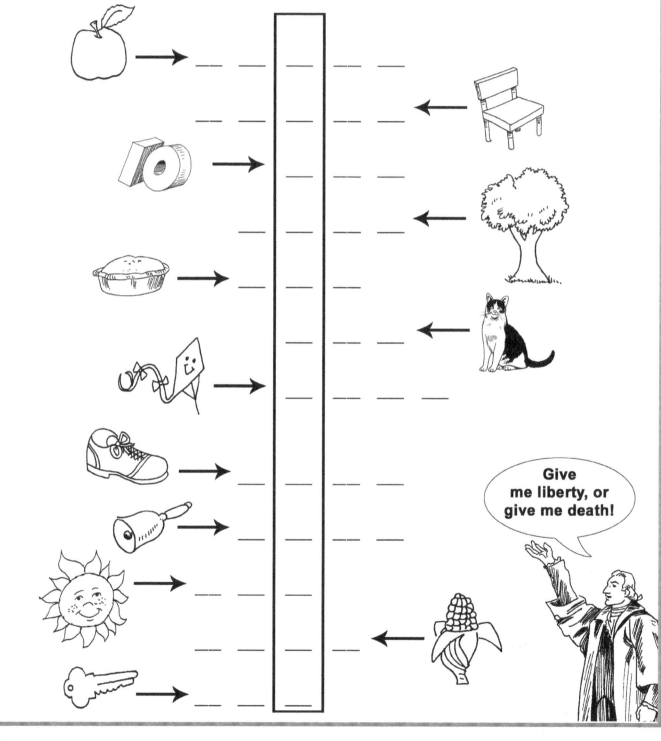

Penman

Credited as the author of the document's preamble, this statesman
is referred to as the "Penman of the Constitution."
To learn his name, first write the opposite of each word. The numbered letters,
when written in their correct spaces below, will spell out the answer.

CLOUDY   ___ ___ ___ ___ ___
          9

LEFT   ___ ___ ___ ___ ___
     10   15   1

ODD   ___ ___ ___ ___
     8   4   7

SQUARE   ___ ___ ___ ___ ___
     6   12   3

EXPORT   ___ ___ ___ ___ ___ ___
       11   2   14

LOWER   ___ ___ ___ ___ ___
   13   16   5

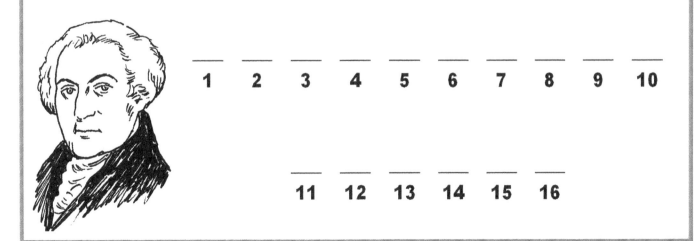

___ ___ ___ ___ ___ ___ ___ ___ ___ ___
1   2   3   4   5   6   7   8   9   10

___ ___ ___ ___ ___ ___
11   12   13   14   15   16

PHILADELPHIA

Where in Philadelphia, Pennsylvania, was the Constitution written and signed?
Find and circle the names of some of the signers in this puzzle.
(The names can appear horizontally, vertically, diagonally, and backwards.)
The letters that remain, once listed in the order they
appear, will complete the answer below.

BEDFORD
BLAIR
BROOM
BUTLER
FEW
KING
LANGDON
MORRIS
WILSON

```
A S S S E M B L
Y I R O O M S F
T R A T E H O E
D R E L T U B W
R O U G S E I I
O M N N R D B L
F E P I E N R S
D D A K E N O O
E L A N G D O N
B C E H A L M L
```

THE _ _ _ _ _ _ _ _ _ _

OF THE PENNSYLVANIA

_ _ _ _ _ _ _ _ _

(TODAY KNOWN AS

_ _ _ _ _ _ _ _ _ _ _ _ _ _ _ _ _ _ _ _ _).

Population

When the Constitution was signed, what was the population of
the United States?

Drop a letter from every word in column A to complete a new word in
column B. Write the dropped letter in column C to learn the answer.

A	B	C
FOUR	O _ _	_
TONE	_ E N	_
RUDE	_ E D	_
TRADE	D _ T E	_
MANY	A _ _	_
TIME	_ E _	_
CLUE	C _ _ _	_
LAST	S _ _	_
TILE	_ E _	_
POET	_ E _	_
NICE	_ C _	_

Preamble

The Preamble to the U.S. Constitution is a brief introduction explaining the Constitution's fundamental purposes and guiding principles.
Use the chart below to decode the following statement.

10	19	13	26	8	17	22	5	24	15	1	21	6
A	B	C	D	E	F	G	H	I	J	K	L	M
2	16	7	12	23	4	20	11	9	18	25	3	14
N	O	P	Q	R	S	T	U	V	W	X	Y	Z

18 8 — 20 5 8 — 7 8 16 7 21 8
(WE THE PEOPLE)

16 17 — 20 5 8 — 11 2 24 20 8 26
(OF THE UNITED)

4 20 10 20 8 4 , 24 2
(STATES, IN)

16 23 26 8 23 — 20 16 — 17 16 23 6
(ORDER TO FORM)

10 — 6 16 23 8 — 7 8 23 17 8 13 20
(A MORE PERFECT)

11 2 24 16 2 ,
(UNION,)

8 4 20 10 19 21 24 4 5
(ESTABLISH)

15 11 4 20 24 13 8 , — 24 2 4 11 23 8
(JUSTICE, INSURE)

26 16 6 8 4 20 24 13
(DOMESTIC)

20 23 10 2 12 11 24 21 24 20 3 ,
(TRANQUILITY,)

7 23 16 9 24 26 8 — 17 16 23 — 20 5 8
(PROVIDE FOR THE)

$$\overline{13}\ \overline{16}\ \overline{6}\ \overline{6}\ \overline{16}\ \overline{2}\qquad \overline{26}\ \overline{8}\ \overline{17}\ \overline{8}\ \overline{2}\ \overline{13}\ \overline{8}\ ,$$

$$\overline{7}\ \overline{23}\ \overline{16}\ \overline{6}\ \overline{16}\ \overline{20}\ \overline{8}\qquad \overline{20}\ \overline{5}\ \overline{8}$$

$$\overline{22}\ \overline{8}\ \overline{2}\ \overline{8}\ \overline{23}\ \overline{10}\ \overline{21}\qquad \overline{18}\ \overline{8}\ \overline{21}\ \overline{17}\ \overline{10}\ \overline{23}\ \overline{8}\ ,$$

$$\overline{10}\ \overline{2}\ \overline{26}\qquad \overline{4}\ \overline{8}\ \overline{13}\ \overline{11}\ \overline{23}\ \overline{8}\qquad \overline{20}\ \overline{5}\ \overline{8}$$

$$\overline{19}\ \overline{21}\ \overline{8}\ \overline{4}\ \overline{4}\ \overline{24}\ \overline{2}\ \overline{22}\ \overline{4}\qquad \overline{16}\ \overline{17}$$

$$\overline{21}\ \overline{24}\ \overline{19}\ \overline{8}\ \overline{23}\ \overline{20}\ \overline{3}\qquad \overline{20}\ \overline{16}$$

$$\overline{16}\ \overline{11}\ \overline{23}\ \overline{4}\ \overline{8}\ \overline{21}\ \overline{9}\ \overline{8}\ \overline{4}\qquad \overline{10}\ \overline{2}\ \overline{26}$$

$$\overline{16}\ \overline{11}\ \overline{23}\qquad \overline{7}\ \overline{16}\ \overline{4}\ \overline{20}\ \overline{8}\ \overline{23}\ \overline{24}\ \overline{20}\ \overline{3}\ ,$$

$$\overline{26}\ \overline{16}\qquad \overline{16}\ \overline{23}\ \overline{26}\ \overline{10}\ \overline{24}\ \overline{2}\qquad \overline{10}\ \overline{2}\ \overline{26}$$

$$\overline{8}\ \overline{4}\ \overline{20}\ \overline{10}\ \overline{19}\ \overline{21}\ \overline{24}\ \overline{4}\ \overline{5}\qquad \overline{20}\ \overline{5}\ \overline{24}\ \overline{4}$$

$$\overline{13}\ \overline{16}\ \overline{2}\ \overline{4}\ \overline{20}\ \overline{24}\ \overline{20}\ \overline{11}\ \overline{20}\ \overline{24}\ \overline{16}\ \overline{2}\qquad \overline{17}\ \overline{16}\ \overline{23}$$

$$\overline{20}\ \overline{5}\ \overline{8}\qquad \overline{11}\ \overline{2}\ \overline{24}\ \overline{20}\ \overline{8}\ \overline{26}\qquad \overline{4}\ \overline{20}\ \overline{10}\ \overline{20}\ \overline{8}\ \overline{4}$$

$$\overline{16}\ \overline{17}\qquad \overline{10}\ \overline{6}\ \overline{8}\ \overline{23}\ \overline{24}\ \overline{13}\ \overline{10}\ .$$

Standing Guard

The delegates discussed and debated the new Constitution all through the summer of 1787. Even though the weather was very warm, windows and doors to the State House were kept closed to ensure privacy. Armed sentries stood guard outside!
Which sentry is different? Find and circle him.

SUPREME LAW OF THE LAND

How did the Constituion make the United States a nation?
Write the names of these objects in their spaces to the right. Then place the
numbered letters in the correct spaces below to complete the answer.

| 1 | 24 | 2 | 14 | 6 |

| 20 | 21 | 4 | 8 | 23 | 12 |

| 3 | 9 | 10 | 11 | 16 |

| 19 | 13 | 15 | 22 | 17 | 18 | 5 | 7 |

THE   CONSTITUTION   ESTABLISHED

__ __ V __ __ __ M __ N __   A N D
1 2   3 4 5   6   7

T H E   __ __ __ __ __ S   A N D
        8 9 10 11 12

__ I __ __ R __ I E S   O F
13   14 15   16

T __ E   __ M __ R I __ __ N
  17   18   19   20 21

__ E __ P __ E .
22   23   24

27

Thirteenth Amendment

From 1804 to 1865, there were no amendments added to the Constitution. This changed when the 13th Amendment was added after the American Civil War. This was the longest period in American history in which there were no changes to the Constitution.

What does the 13th Amendment do?

Circle every 4th letter in the puzzle below. These letters, when listed, will spell out the answer.

T	C	E	A	M	D	O
B	G	L	U	O	S	E
A	L	N	P	R	I	F
H	J	S	K	Q	V	H
C	O	N	S	U	I	O

L	N	Y	H	A	R	Y	W	V
T	R	U	E	I	O	A	R	E

	C	N	Y

__ __ __ __ __ __

__ __ __ __ __ __

Three Branches

The U.S. Constitution divides our government into three branches. Answer each clue below. The numbered letters, when written in their correct spaces, will form the names of these branches.

INDEPENDENCE DAY MONTH	— — — — 9 10 1 14
MIDDLE OF THE WEEK	W __ __ N __ __ __ __ Y 2 11 2 5 11 6
OPPOSITE OF TAKE	__ __ __ E 3 4 8
ADULT KITTEN	__ A __ 12 7
PERSON WITH SPECIAL ABILITY	E __ P E __ T 15 13

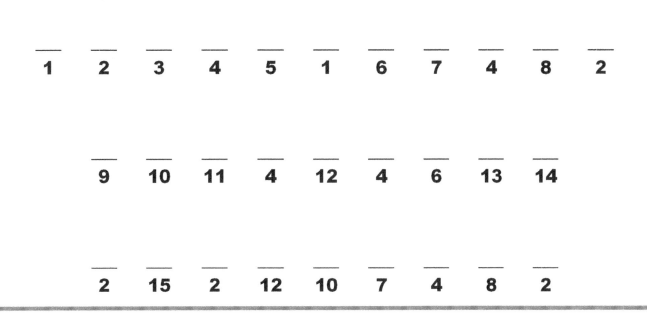

— — — — — — — — — — — —
1   2   3   4   5   1   6   7   4   8   2

— — — — — — — — —
9   10   11   4   12   4   6   13   14

— — — — — — — — —
2   15   2   12   10   7   4   8   2

Veteran Signer

Who was the oldest American to sign the Constitution at the age of 81?
Take each letter through this maze to reveal the answer.

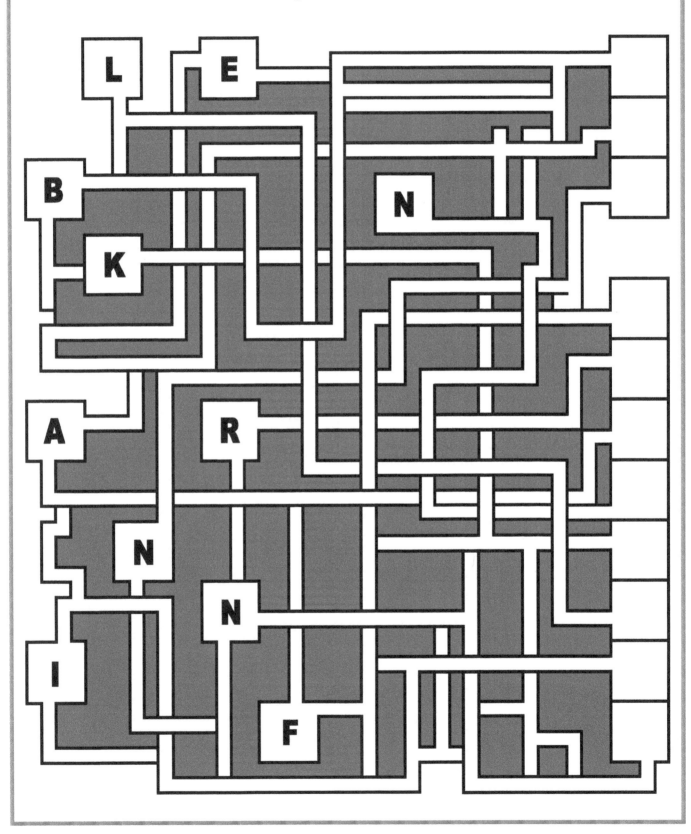

What's the Difference?

Both the Declaration of Independence and the Constitution played important roles in American history.

To learn more about each document, fill in each blank with the letter of the alphabet that comes BEFORE each letter below it.

Declaration of Independence (1776):

A _STATEMENT_ _ADOPTED_ BY
　　T U B U F N F O U　　B E P Q U F E

THE _SECOND_ _CONTINENTAL_
　　　T F D P O E　　D P O U J O F O U B M

CONGRESS _ANNOUNCING_
　　　　　B O O P V O D J O H

THAT THE 13 _AMERICAN_
　　　　　　　B N F S J D B O

COLONIES REGARDED
D P M P O J F T

THEMSELVES _INDEPENDENT_
　　　　　　　J O E F Q F O E F O U

FROM _BRITISH_ _RULE_ .
　　　C S J U J T I　　S V M F

Constitution (1787):

THE _SUPREME_ _LAW_ OF THE
　　　T V Q S F N F　　M B X

USA , IT IS THE _FIRST_
V T B　　　　　　　　　G J S T U

CONSTITUTION _OF_ _ITS_
　　　　　　　　　P G　　J U T

KIND AND _HAS_ _INFLUENCED_
L J O E　　　　　I B T　　J O G M V F O D F E

THE CONSTITUTIONS _OF_
　　　　　　　　　　　　　P G

OTHER _NATIONS_ .
　　　　O B U J P O T

31

What's the Difference?

Find and circle ten things that are different between these two pictures of some of the delgates discussing the Constitution.

Of the forty-two delegates who attended most of the meetings, thirty-nine actually signed the Constitution.

Which Two?

Which two future U.S. Presidents signed the Constitution?
Travel through this two-page maze to discover the answer.

Words

The Constitution has 4,400 words.
How many words can you form using only the letters
from the word
CONSTITUTION ?

Amendments

In 1791, Congress ratified 10 amendments (or changes) to the Constitution that outlined the basic rights and freedoms of American citizens. What is the term for these amendments? Circle all the letters that contain a star ✷. Then list these letters, in the order they appear, in the spaces below to form the answer.

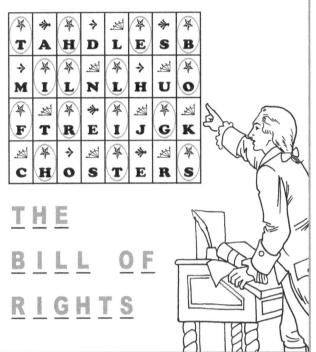

T H E

B I L L   O F

R I G H T S

Articles

The Constitution is divided into seven articles, or sections, each addressing a different topic. Find and circle the listed words having to do with these articles in the puzzle below. (The words can appear horizontally, vertically, diagonally, and backwards.)

BILLS
BRANCH
COMMERCE
CONGRESS
EXECUTIVE
FEDERAL
GUIDELINES
HOUSE
JUDICIAL
LEGISLATIVE
OATH
POWER
PRESIDENT
PROTECT
SENATE
STATES
SUPPORT
SUPREME COURT
VOTE

Before the Constitution

In 1776, the 13 colonies declared themselves free from Great Britain and became the United States of America. The young country initially developed a document that served as its first constitution. What was it called? Unscramble a synonym for each of these words. (Synonyms are words that mean nearly the same thing, like JOYOUS and MERRY.) Once you have unscrambled them, write the numbered letters in their correct order below to complete the answer.

HALT ☞ TOSP   S T O P
                11 1 25

SHOW ☞ LISDPYA   D I S P L A Y
                  19 7 9 22

QUIET ☞ LEEPACUF   P E A C E F U L
                    20 4 14 3 13

BENT ☞ ORKEDCO   C R O O K E D
                  8 21 12 15 10

CORRECT ☞ IGTRH   R I G H T
                   5 24 2 6

HUMOROUS ☞ YFNUN   F U N N Y
                    17 26 16

TINY ☞ ETTILL   L I T T L E
                 23   18

T H E   A R T I C L E S   O F
1 2 3   4 5 6 7 8 9 10 11   12 13

C O N F E D E R A T I O N
14 15 16 17 18 19 20 21 22 23 24 25 26

Constitution Day

Constitution Day is normally celebrated on September 17. When it falls on a weekend or on a holiday, schools and other institutions observe the holiday on an adjacent weekday. Although first recognized in 1911, what year was Constitution Day established by law? Using a pencil, darken in the areas that contain a dot ● to reveal the answer.

FAMOUS SIGNERS

Signers of the Constitution included some of the greatest names in early American history.
Correctly travel through this maze to reach the person who did NOT sign.

BENJAMIN FRANKLIN

GEORGE WASHINGTON

THOMAS JEFFERSON

JAMES MADISON

Page 5

Federalist Papers

James Madison and Alexander Hamilton wrote a series of essays to persuade people to approve the Constitution. The 85 essays, published in newspapers across the states in 1787, were known as the "Federalist Papers." Which statesman and patriot from New York City helped Madison and Hamilton write these articles?
To learn his name, cross out each letter that appears THREE times in this puzzle grid. List the remaining letters, in the order they appear, in the blank spaces below.

J<u>O</u>H<u>N</u> J<u>A</u>Y

<u>J O H N</u>   <u>J A Y</u>

Page 6

First American

One of the Founding Fathers of the U.S., Benjamin Franklin was an author, printer, politician, postmaster, inventor, and scientist. He earned the title of "The First American" for his devoted work in uniting the colonies in the years leading up to the Revolutionary War. Franklin is one of the few Fathers who signed both the Declaration of Independence and the Constitution.
Fill in this wall by using only the letters in the top name BEN to complete the 10 words below. Some letters may be used more than once in a word.

B	E	N
B	E	A	N
B	O	N	E
B	E	I	N	G
B	L	E	N	D
B	R	O	K	E	N
B	E	T	W	E	E	N
B	E	N	E	F	I	T
B	E	N	E	A	T	H
S	U	N	B	E	A	M
C	R	A	N	B	E	R	R	Y

Page 7

First National Thanksgiving

A proclamation by President George Washington and a congressional resolution established the first national Thanksgiving Day on Nov. 26, 1789.
What was the reason for the holiday?
Use the chart below to decode the answer.

It had nothing to do with pumpkin pie!

	a	b	c	d	e	f
1	G	K	O	H	R	B
2	S	A	F	I	W	U
3	E	T	V	N	C	J

<u>T O</u>   <u>G I V E</u>
3b 1c   1a 2d 3c 3a

<u>T H A N K S</u>   <u>F O R</u>
3b 1d 2b 3d 1b 2a   2c 1c 1e

<u>T H E</u>   <u>N E W</u>
3b 1d 3a   3d 3a 2e

<u>C O N S T I T U T I O N</u> .
3e 1c 3d 2a 3b 2d 3b 2f 3b 2d 1c 3d

Page 8

First State

Which was the first state to ratify the Constitution?
Write the names of these U.S. states in their correct spaces. The circled letters, once listed below in the order they appear, will spell out the answer.

ALASKA
CALIFORNIA
MAINE
MONTANA
NEW HAMPSHIRE
RHODE ISLAND

December 7, 1787

D E L A W A R E

Framers

The delegates present at the Constitutional Convention were also referred to as Framers of the Constitution.
Draw a line from each picture on the left to its twin on the right.

Influential Delegate

Representing New York, this writer, lawyer and Revolutionary War soldier was just 30 years old when he signed the Constitution. One of the most influential interpreters and promoters of the document, he later served as the first U.S. Secretary of the Treasury.
To learn his name, first circle these words in the puzzle below. The letters that remain, once listed in the order they appear, will spell out his name.

AMBITIOUS   ASSEMBLYMAN   BRAVE
CAREER   DELEGATE   HUSBAND
LAWYER   LEADER   MILITARY
PATRIOT   POLITICIAN   SMART
SOLDIER   TRUE   WRITER

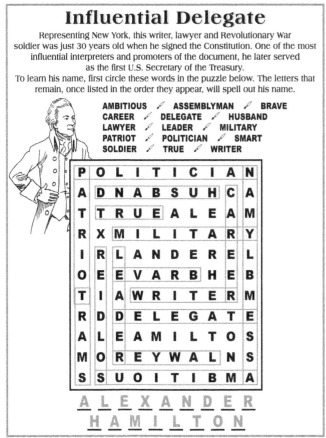

A L E X A N D E R
H A M I L T O N

In the Beginning

Although Americans celebrate the fourth of July and the signing of the Declaration of Independence as the beginning of our country, the real birth of our nation took place in 1787.
Circle the EVEN numbered letters in this puzzle. Then list these letters, in the order they appear, in the spaces below to complete the sentence.

16	5	4	22	11	6	3	14	20	13	2
D	A	E	L	I	E	B	G	A	S	T
21	8	31	10	24	12	18	1	7	26	9
R	E	Y	S	C	O	U	M	H	N	D
16	8	14	7	6	11	12	4	10	29	2
T	R	Y	F	G	P	A	T	H	W	E
28	1	32	12	5	22	26	3	8	16	30
R	V	E	D	K	C	O	L	N	S	T
2	10	4	7	12	11	6	16	15	8	13
I	T	U	Q	T	A	I	O	E	N	S

ON   SEPTEMBER   17,   1787

DELEGATES   FROM   ALL

OVER   THE   COUNTRY

GATHERED   TO   SIGN

THE   CONSTITUTION

OF   THE   UNITED   STATES.

Jacob Shallus

The Constitution was "penned" by a Pennsylvania General Assembly clerk named Jacob Shallus. An engrosser (or penman), Shallus handwrote the 4-page document onto parchment over the course of one weekend.
How much was he paid?
Fill in the areas that contain this symbol ♣ to reveal the answer.

JAMES MADISON

James Madison is often referred to as the "Father of the Constitution" because many of his ideas made their way into the document. A statesman and political theorist, he later served as America's 4th president.
Which two pictures of James Madison are exactly the same?
Find and circle them.

Lawyer and Statesman

A Founding Father of the United States, this representative from Connecticut was the only person to sign all four great state papers of the U.S.: the Continental Association, the Declaration of Independence, the Articles of Confederation, and the Constitution.
To learn his name, write the listed words into the grid in alphabetical order. The third letter from each word will spell out his name.

JUST
EGGS
TINY
PART
CART
HURT
SAME
KOHL
DOOR
SEAL
MEET
FREE

C	A	R	T
D	O	O	R
E	G	G	S
F	R	E	E
H	U	R	T
J	U	S	T
K	O	H	L
M	E	E	T
P	A	R	T
S	A	M	E
S	E	A	L
T	I	N	Y

Madison's Plan

While waiting for the Convention to formally begin in Philadelphia, James Madison sketched out his initial draft of the Constitution. What was it called?
Travel through this maze to discover the answer.

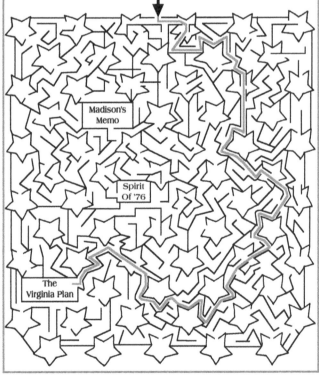

Madison's Memo

Spirit Of '76

The Virginia Plan

Not Born in the USA

Representing New Jersey, this signer of the U.S. Constitution was born in County Antrim, Ireland. When he was almost 2 years of age, his family emigrated to America.
Correctly travel through this maze to discover his name.

| William Livingston | William Paterson | William C. Houston |

Official Start

The government under the U.S. Constitution officially began on what date? Travel through this maze by choosing the path made up of only letters from the word CONSTITUTION.

July 4, 1789

March 4, 1789

June 4, 1789

April 4, 1789

On Display

Since 1952, the original Constitution has been kept on display. It is preserved in a case that contains argon gas and is kept at 67 degrees Fahrenheit. To find out where this historical document is located, fill in the blanks with their correct missing vowels,
A E I O U.

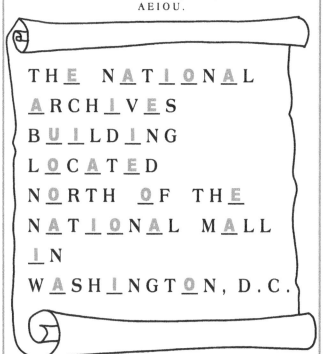

THE NATIONAL
ARCHIVES
BUILDING
LOCATED
NORTH OF THE
NATIONAL MALL
IN
WASHINGTON, D.C.

Opposed the Constitution

Best known for his speeches about independence, this Founding Father surprisingly did NOT sign the Constitution. He feared it endangered the rights of states as well as the freedoms of individuals. (He did later help gain approval for the Bill of Rights.)
Write the name of each object pictured. One letter from each will spell out his name.

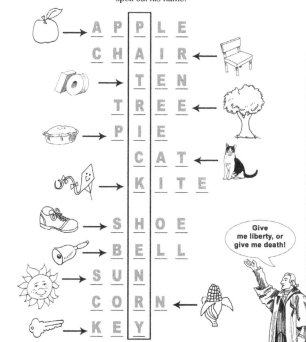

APPLE
CHAIR
TEN
TREE
PIE
CAT
KITE
SHOE
BELL
SUN
CORN
KEY

Give me liberty, or give me death!

Penman

Credited as the author of the document's preamble, this statesman is referred to as the "Penman of the Constitution."
To learn his name, first write the opposite of each word. The numbered letters, when written in their correct spaces below, will spell out the answer.

CLOUDY   S U_9_ N N Y

LEFT   R_10_ I G_15_ H T_1_

ODD   E_8_ V_4_ E N_7_

SQUARE   R_6_ O U_12_ N_3_ D

EXPORT   I_11_ M P_2_ O R T_14_

LOWER   R A_13_ I S_16_ E_5_

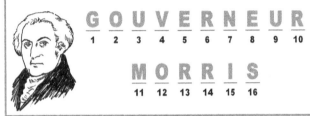

G O U V E R N E U R
1 2 3 4 5 6 7 8 9 10

M O R R I S
11 12 13 14 15 16

Page 21

PHILADELPHIA

Where in Philadelphia, Pennsylvania, was the Constitution written and signed?
Find and circle the names of some of the signers in this puzzle.
(The names can appear horizontally, vertically, diagonally, and backwards.)
The letters that remain, once listed in the order they appear, will complete the answer below.

BEDFORD
BLAIR
BROOM
BUTLER
FEW
KING
LANGDON
MORRIS
WILSON

```
A S S E M B L
Y I R O O M S F
T R A T E H O E
D R E L T U B W
R O U G S E I I
O M N N R D B L
F E P I E N R S
D D A K E N O O
E L A N G D O N
B C E H A L M L
```

THE A S S E M B L Y   R O O M

OF THE PENNSYLVANIA

S T A T E   H O U S E

(TODAY KNOWN AS

I N D E P E N D E N C E   H A L L).

Page 22

Population

When the Constitution was signed, what was the population of the United States?
Drop a letter from every word in column A to complete a new word in column B. Write the dropped letter in column C to learn the answer.

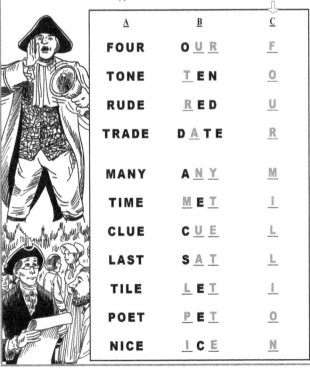

	A	B	C
	FOUR	O U R	F
	TONE	T E N	O
	RUDE	R E D	U
	TRADE	D A T E	R
	MANY	A N Y	M
	TIME	M E T	I
	CLUE	C U E	L
	LAST	S A T	L
	TILE	L E T	I
	POET	P E T	O
	NICE	I C E	N

Page 23

Preamble

The Preamble to the U.S. Constitution is a brief introduction explaining the Constitution's fundamental purposes and guiding principles.
Use the chart below to decode the following statement.

10	19	13	26	8	17	22	5	24	15	1	21	6
A	B	C	D	E	F	G	H	I	J	K	L	M

2	16	7	12	23	4	20	11	9	18	25	3	14
N	O	P	Q	R	S	T	U	V	W	X	Y	Z

W E   T H E   P E O P L E
18 8   20 5 8   7 8 16 7 21 8

O F   T H E   U N I T E D
16 17   20 5 8   11 2 24 20 8 26

S T A T E S ,   I N
4 20 10 20 8 4   24 2

O R D E R   T O   F O R M
16 23 26 8 23   20 16   17 16 23 6

A   M O R E   P E R F E C T
10   6 16 23 8   7 8 23 17 8 13 20

U N I O N ,
11 2 24 16 2

E S T A B L I S H
8 4 20 10 19 21 24 4 5

J U S T I C E ,   I N S U R E
15 11 4 20 24 13 8   24 2 4 11 23 8

D O M E S T I C
26 16 6 8 4 20 24 13

T R A N Q U I L I T Y ,
20 23 10 2 12 11 24 21 24 20 3

P R O V I D E   F O R   T H E
7 23 16 9 24 26 8   17 16 23   20 5 8

Page 24

42

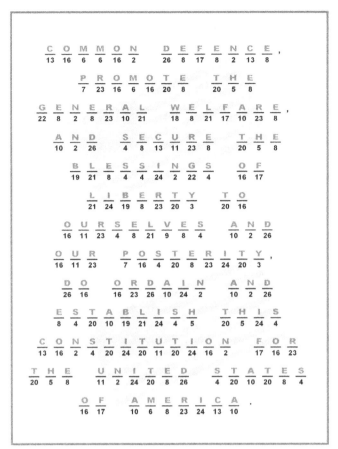

$$\underset{13}{C}\;\underset{16}{O}\;\underset{6}{M}\;\underset{6}{M}\;\underset{16}{O}\;\underset{2}{N}\qquad \underset{26}{D}\;\underset{8}{E}\;\underset{17}{F}\;\underset{8}{E}\;\underset{2}{N}\;\underset{13}{C}\;\underset{8}{E}\;,$$

$$\underset{7}{P}\;\underset{23}{R}\;\underset{16}{O}\;\underset{6}{M}\;\underset{16}{O}\;\underset{20}{T}\;\underset{8}{E}\qquad \underset{20}{T}\;\underset{5}{H}\;\underset{8}{E}$$

$$\underset{22}{G}\;\underset{8}{E}\;\underset{2}{N}\;\underset{8}{E}\;\underset{23}{R}\;\underset{10}{A}\;\underset{21}{L}\qquad \underset{18}{W}\;\underset{8}{E}\;\underset{21}{L}\;\underset{17}{F}\;\underset{10}{A}\;\underset{23}{R}\;\underset{8}{E}\;,$$

$$\underset{10}{A}\;\underset{2}{N}\;\underset{26}{D}\qquad \underset{4}{S}\;\underset{8}{E}\;\underset{13}{C}\;\underset{11}{U}\;\underset{23}{R}\;\underset{8}{E}\qquad \underset{20}{T}\;\underset{5}{H}\;\underset{8}{E}$$

$$\underset{19}{B}\;\underset{21}{L}\;\underset{8}{E}\;\underset{4}{S}\;\underset{4}{S}\;\underset{24}{I}\;\underset{2}{N}\;\underset{22}{G}\;\underset{4}{S}\qquad \underset{16}{O}\;\underset{17}{F}$$

$$\underset{21}{L}\;\underset{24}{I}\;\underset{19}{B}\;\underset{8}{E}\;\underset{23}{R}\;\underset{20}{T}\;\underset{3}{Y}\qquad \underset{20}{T}\;\underset{16}{O}$$

$$\underset{16}{O}\;\underset{11}{U}\;\underset{23}{R}\;\underset{4}{S}\;\underset{8}{E}\;\underset{21}{L}\;\underset{9}{V}\;\underset{8}{E}\;\underset{4}{S}\qquad \underset{10}{A}\;\underset{2}{N}\;\underset{26}{D}$$

$$\underset{16}{O}\;\underset{11}{U}\;\underset{23}{R}\qquad \underset{7}{P}\;\underset{16}{O}\;\underset{4}{S}\;\underset{20}{T}\;\underset{8}{E}\;\underset{23}{R}\;\underset{24}{I}\;\underset{20}{T}\;\underset{3}{Y}\;,$$

$$\underset{26}{D}\;\underset{16}{O}\qquad \underset{16}{O}\;\underset{23}{R}\;\underset{26}{D}\;\underset{10}{A}\;\underset{24}{I}\;\underset{2}{N}\qquad \underset{10}{A}\;\underset{2}{N}\;\underset{26}{D}$$

$$\underset{8}{E}\;\underset{4}{S}\;\underset{20}{T}\;\underset{10}{A}\;\underset{19}{B}\;\underset{21}{L}\;\underset{24}{I}\;\underset{4}{S}\;\underset{5}{H}\qquad \underset{20}{T}\;\underset{5}{H}\;\underset{24}{I}\;\underset{4}{S}$$

$$\underset{13}{C}\;\underset{16}{O}\;\underset{2}{N}\;\underset{4}{S}\;\underset{20}{T}\;\underset{24}{I}\;\underset{20}{T}\;\underset{11}{U}\;\underset{20}{T}\;\underset{24}{I}\;\underset{16}{O}\;\underset{2}{N}\qquad \underset{17}{F}\;\underset{16}{O}\;\underset{23}{R}$$

$$\underset{20}{T}\;\underset{5}{H}\;\underset{8}{E}\qquad \underset{11}{U}\;\underset{2}{N}\;\underset{24}{I}\;\underset{20}{T}\;\underset{8}{E}\;\underset{26}{D}\qquad \underset{4}{S}\;\underset{20}{T}\;\underset{10}{A}\;\underset{20}{T}\;\underset{8}{E}\;\underset{4}{S}$$

$$\underset{16}{O}\;\underset{17}{F}\qquad \underset{10}{A}\;\underset{6}{M}\;\underset{8}{E}\;\underset{23}{R}\;\underset{24}{I}\;\underset{13}{C}\;\underset{10}{A}\;.$$

Page 25

Standing Guard

The delegates discussed and debated the new Constitution all through the summer of 1787. Even though the weather was very warm, windows and doors to the State House were kept closed to ensure privacy. Armed sentries stood guard outside! Which sentry is different? Find and circle him.

Page 26

SUPREME LAW OF THE LAND

How did the Constitution make the United States a nation? Write the names of these objects in their spaces to the right. Then place the numbered letters in the correct spaces below to complete the answer.

→ $\underset{1}{G}\;\underset{24}{L}\;\underset{2}{O}\;\underset{14}{B}\;\underset{6}{E}$

→ $\underset{20}{C}\;\underset{21}{A}\;\underset{4}{R}\;\underset{8}{R}\;\underset{23}{O}\;\underset{12}{T}$

→ $\underset{3}{E}\;\underset{9}{I}\;\underset{10}{G}\;\underset{11}{H}\;\underset{16}{T}$

→ $\underset{19}{E}\;\underset{13}{L}\;\underset{15}{E}\;\underset{22}{P}\;\underset{17}{H}\;\underset{18}{A}\;\underset{5}{N}\;\underset{7}{T}$

THE CONSTITUTION ESTABLISHED

$\underset{1}{G}\;\underset{2}{O}\;V\;\underset{3}{E}\;\underset{4}{R}\;\underset{5}{N}\;M\;\underset{6}{E}\;\underset{7}{N}\;T$ AND

THE $\underset{8}{R}\;\underset{9}{I}\;\underset{10}{G}\;\underset{11}{H}\;\underset{12}{T}$ S AND

$\underset{13}{L}\;I\;\underset{14}{B}\;\underset{15}{E}\;\underset{16}{R}\;T\;I$ E S OF

T $\underset{17}{H}$ E $\underset{18}{A}\;\underset{19}{M}$ E R I $\underset{20}{C}\;\underset{21}{A}$ N

$\underset{22}{P}$ E $\underset{23}{O}$ P $\underset{24}{L}$ E .

Page 27

Thirteenth Amendment

From 1804 to 1865, there were no amendments added to the Constitution. This changed when the 13th Amendment was added after the American Civil War. This was the longest period in American history in which there were no changes to the Constitution.
What does the 13th Amendment do?
Circle every 4th letter in the puzzle below. These letters, when listed, will spell out the answer.

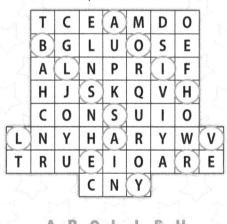

T	C	E	A	M	D	O
B	G	L	U	O	S	E
A	L	N	P	R	I	F
H	J	S	K	Q	V	H
C	O	N	S	U	I	O
L	N	Y	H	A	R	Y	W	V
T	R	U	E	I	O	A	R	E
		C	N	Y	

$\underline{A}\;\underline{B}\;\underline{O}\;\underline{L}\;\underline{I}\;\underline{S}\;\underline{H}$

$\underline{S}\;\underline{L}\;\underline{A}\;\underline{V}\;\underline{E}\;\underline{R}\;\underline{Y}$

Page 28

Three Branches

The U.S. Constitution divides our government into three branches.
Answer each clue below. The numbered letters, when written in their correct spaces, will form the names of these branches.

| INDEPENDENCE DAY MONTH | J U L Y |
| | 9 10 1 14 |

| MIDDLE OF THE WEEK | W E D N E S D A Y |
| | 2 11 2 5 11 6 |

| OPPOSITE OF TAKE | G I V E |
| | 3 4 8 |

| ADULT KITTEN | C A T |
| | 12 7 |

| PERSON WITH SPECIAL ABILITY | E X P E R T |
| | 15 13 |

L E G I S L A T I V E
1 2 3 4 5 1 6 7 4 8 2

J U D I C I A R Y
9 10 11 4 12 4 6 13 14

E X E C U T I V E
2 15 2 12 10 7 4 8 2

Veteran Signer

Who was the oldest American to sign the Constitution at the age of 81?
Take each letter through this maze to reveal the answer.

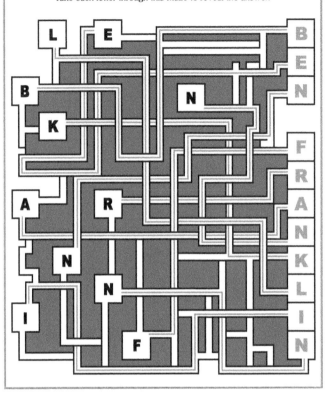

What's the Difference?

Both the Declaration of Independence and the Constitution played important roles in American history.
To learn more about each document, fill in each blank with the letter of the alphabet that comes BEFORE each letter below it.

Declaration of Independence (1776):

A S T A T E M E N T A D O P T E D B Y
T U B U F N F O U B E P Q U F E

T H E S E C O N D C O N T I N E N T A L
T F D P O E D P O U J O F O U B M

C O N G R E S S A N N O U N C I N G
B O O P V O D J O H

T H A T T H E 1 3 A M E R I C A N
B N F S J D B O

C O L O N I E S R E G A R D E D
D P M P O J F T

T H E M S E L V E S I N D E P E N D E N T
J O E F Q F O E F O U

F R O M B R I T I S H R U L E .
C S J U J T I S V M F

Constitution (1787):

T H E S U P R E M E L A W O F T H E
T V Q S F N F M B X

U S A , I T I S T H E F I R S T
V T B G J S T U

C O N S T I T U T I O N O F I T S
P G J U T

K I N D A N D H A S I N F L U E N C E D
L J O E I B T J O G M V F O D F E

T H E C O N S T I T U T I O N S O F
P G

O T H E R N A T I O N S .
O B U J P O T

Of the forty-two delegates who attended most of the meetings, thirty-nine actually signed the Constitution.

Which Two?

Which two future U.S. Presidents signed the Constitution?
Travel through this two-page maze to discover the answer.

JOHN ADAMS
SECOND PRESIDENT

THOMAS JEFFERSON
THIRD PRESIDENT

JAMES MONROE
FIFTH PRESIDENT

JOHN QUINCY ADAMS
SIXTH PRESIDENT

GEORGE WASHINGTON
FIRST PRESIDENT

JAMES MADISON
FOURTH PRESIDENT

Words

The Constitution has 4,400 words.
How many words can you form using only the letters
from the word
CONSTITUTION ?

Here are just some words:

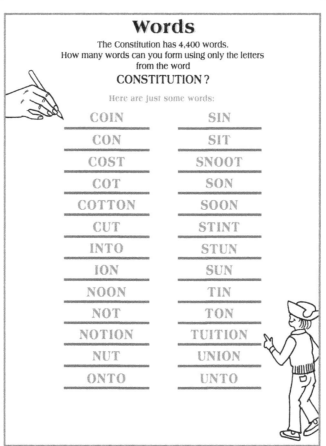

COIN	SIN
CON	SIT
COST	SNOOT
COT	SON
COTTON	SOON
CUT	STINT
INTO	STUN
ION	SUN
NOON	TIN
NOT	TON
NOTION	TUITION
NUT	UNION
ONTO	UNTO